Lions

angus

This edition published in 2004
by Angus Books Ltd
12 Ravensbury Terrace
London SW18 4RL

ISBN 1-904594-61-1

OR BROWN PARTWORKS LIMITED
Author: John Woodward
Consultant: Dr. Adrian Seymour
Project editor: Tim Harris
Managing editor: Anne O'Daly
Picture research: Adrian Bentley
Index: Margaret Mitchell

PICTURE CREDITS
Artworks: AntBits Illustration
Bruce Coleman Collection: (Bruce Coleman Inc.) 25; (Christer Fredriksson) 10, 23 above; (Dr Eckart Pott) 19; (Erwin & Peggy Bauer) 26; (Gerald S. Cubitt) 7 above, 27; (Johnny Johnson) contents page, 8. *Image Bank:* (Joseph van Os) 4, 17, 20–21. *NHPA:* (Ann & Steve Toon) 23 below; (Daryl Balfour) 15 above; (Dr Eckart Pott) 12–13; (John Shaw) 6; (Martin Harvey) 16–17, 18, 24; (Nigel J. Dennis) 9 above, 9 below; (Stephen Krasemann) 5 above, 11, 29. *Still Pictures:* (Bojan Brecelj) 28–29; (M. & C. Denis-Huot) 14; (Michael Fairchild) 5 below; (Nicolas Granier) 7 below; (Nigel J. Dennis) title page; (Yann Arthus-Bertrand) front cover, 15 below.

Series created by Brown Partworks Limited.
Designed by Wilson Design Associates

Production by Omnipress,
Eastbourne, UK
Printed and bound in Dubai

Contents

Introduction

Lions are among the best known of all wild animals and have the reputation of being brave and powerful. They are the second largest of the big cats, after the tiger. Armed with huge dagger teeth and slashing claws, a lion is built to hunt. To such a beast a human is just a snack.

What makes lions extra special, though, is the way they live. They are not solitary prowlers, like the tiger and other wild cats. They live in family groups called prides. Lions rear their cubs together, feed together, and hunt together. When a group of lions hunts as a team, it can catch almost anything.

We are going to look at how these lion families spend their lives. This book will tell you how

▼ *With its flowing mane, the male lion is one of the most unmistakable sights on the African plains.*

◄ *A family of lions shelters from the heat in the shade of a tree. Lions have a reputation for being lazy. They rest for 20 hours each day!*

they get on with each other, deal with neighbours, hunt their prey, and bring up their babies. We will see exactly what it is that makes these amazing cats so special, and just why they are admired and feared.

Lazy lions

Pound for pound, meat contains much more energy than plants. While their grass-eating victims have to spend most of their lives eating, lions need to hunt for just three or four hours a day. This means they can spend most of their time lazing around—and that's exactly what they do.

The king of beasts

The majestic lion certainly deserves its title of "king of the beasts." The other big cats dare not cross it, for a lion will kill a lone leopard or cheetah if it gets the chance. If a lion catches a wild dog off-guard, it can toss it in the air like a doll and kill it with a single bite.

The only real threat to the lion's authority is the burly spotted hyena, which hunts in big packs and has massive, bone-cracking jaws. Hyenas often steal lion kills, but then lions also steal hyena kills. The two types of animal are deadly enemies; but if it comes to a fight, the lions usually win.

▼ *A male lion chases away a spotted hyena that may have been trying to steal a meal.*

The pride

Some lions live alone, like other cats, but these lone lions are the unlucky ones. Lions prefer to live in a group, and the most important type of lion society is the pride.

A lion pride is a big family of up to 12 related lionesses (female lions) and their young, plus up to six adult males. The females do nearly all the hunting and work together to look after their cubs. Lionesses may stay in the same pride for life, but the males are driven out by stronger rival males after two to four years. These takeovers can be violent, and the job of the males is to defend the pride against them. While the females hunt for food for the pride, the males fight.

Each pride has its own hunting territory, and the pride is usually scattered all over it in small groups. If prey is scarce, the lions

▲ A pride of lions shares the results of a kill. Some are eating, while others are resting in the shade of a tree. Females provide the food for the rest of the group.

have to roam over a vast area to get enough to eat. Smaller, richer territories are less tiring and easier to defend, so the pride's territory is never any bigger than it needs to be.

However, not all lions live in prides. Some lions are lone wanderers. Lions that live alone are usually old males who have been defeated in battle or young lions who have left the pride.

Lone lions have a tough time. Hunting alone, they cannot tackle large prey animals. They have to hunt across the territory of other lion prides. The owners do not like sharing their ground; and if they meet the intruders, they are likely to attack them.

▼ *Lion populations have a few lone wanderers, especially in places where prey is hard to find.*

◄ *A group of Asian lions rests in the Gir National Park, northwest India.*

Brothers in arms

Young female lions usually stay with their mothers in the pride, but the young males always leave home. Sometimes they go alone, but normally brothers and half-brothers leave in groups. They roam through the territories of other prides. These gangs do so much better than the loners that unrelated lone males often form gangs of their own.

Friends and enemies

Like all animals that live together, lions communicate with each other. They use sound, and they are also very sensitive to touch and facial expressions. Scent is important, especially when lions are claiming their territory.

The most impressive sound made by a lion is its roar, but it can grunt, growl, snarl, hiss, meow, and even purr like a pet cat. By changing the tone and loudness of all these sounds, a lion can signal all kinds of feelings, from contentment to a deadly threat. Lions back up these sounds by nuzzling, rubbing, and licking. They rub their heads in greeting like

▲ *A lion's roar is a warning, telling other male lions to stay away.*

▲ *Two lionesses rub their heads together.*

more than most animals, and they have at least 17 different expressions. For a lion that is really useful because it can check its neighbour's mood before doing anything that might annoy it. Annoying a lion is a serious mistake, even for another lion!

Lions use scent signals like tomcats, marking their territory and sniffing any scent marks left by other lions. They spray strong-smelling urine onto trees, bushes, rocks, and other scent posts. Strange lions who are just passing through find this handy because they can track the movements of the territory owners and keep out of their way.

domestic cats and often lie close together to keep each other warm and for protection.

Lions have surprisingly expressive faces. They can move their lips and face muscles far

The lion's roar

The full-throated roar of a lion is a terrifying sound and can be heard for miles around. Lions probably mean it to be terrifying because they often roar to show other lions who's who. A lion defending his territory, for example, roars loudly to warn off any trespassers. He may also roar at a rival during an argument, hoping to scare off the other lion without needing to fight. Yet lions also roar to call other members of the pride. The whole pride sometimes roars in chorus, often after making a kill, after eating, and around dawn and dusk.

▼ *This lioness is alert to any changes around her. Her eyes scan the grasslands, her ears pick up sounds, and she sniffs the air for familiar and unfamiliar smells.*

Finding a meal

When a lion is hunting alone, it may pounce on anything that moves, even rats and small birds. Lions are more likely to capture prey if they hunt as a group. When lions hunt together, they concentrate on large game like wildebeest, buffalo, and zebra.

They have a problem, though. A lion can sprint at 36 mph (58km/h), but an antelope or zebra can streak away at speeds of up to 50 mph (80km/h). The only way a lion can catch its fast-moving prey is by stalking close enough to spring an ambush. When a pride of lionesses hunts together, it also

▼ *Lions hunt using stealth. A stalking lioness will freeze if her victim looks up.*

fans out and partly encircles the prey to cut off its escape. Lions usually hunt at night; but if there is enough scrub or long grass to provide cover, they will hunt in daylight. When the lions have crept to within 100 ft (30m) or so of their quarry, they strike. Charging at full tilt, they try to knock their victim to the ground before it gets away. Even if one lion fails, another may leap from hiding to finish the job.

The lion sinks its great claws into the animal's back and drags it down with its weight and strength. It sinks its huge dagger teeth into the victim's throat or muzzle to cut off the air supply. The victim soon suffocates, and the lions gather to share the kill.

In a lion pride most of the hunting is done by the lionesses. When it comes to feeding, though, a male can often brush the smaller lionesses aside to grab most of the kill. Luckily, a big animal such as a wildebeest or zebra usually has enough meat on it for the whole pride—including the cubs, who eat last.

▲ *Lionesses work together to bring down a zebra. One lioness has jumped onto the victim's back to pull it to the ground. The others will join in the feast.*

Dead meat

Lions may be expert hunters, but they are scavengers too. They often steal prey killed by hyenas, cheetahs, leopards, and wild dogs. One survey in the Ngorongoro Crater, Tanzania, found that eight out of ten lion "kills" were actually killed by hyenas.

The mating game

Lions can breed all year round. The lionesses are only interested in mating for two to four days every month or so, though. Sometimes they go for months without coming into breeding condition (called estrus), then all the lionesses in the pride are ready to mate at the same time.

The pride males have to be ready to mate whenever the females are ready, and they have to make sure that trespassing males do not mate with the females first. The males within the pride rarely fight over females because they need each other to help defend the pride against intruders. They settle the problem by "claiming" females as they become receptive and guarding them throughout the mating period.

▼ *A male lion approaches a female who is ready to mate. The female doesn't always welcome him!*

Each male can only guard one female at a time. Another male may mate with the female the next time she comes into estrus. As a result, all the pride males usually end up as joint fathers of all the cubs born that season.

Some lion cubs are fathered by strangers who sneak in and mate with females while the pride males are busy elsewhere. If the outsider lions manage this without being spotted by the pride males, their cubs are raised as part of the pride.

▶ *The male can tell if a female is in estrus by her scent. He opens his mouth and wrinkles his nose.*

Blood brothers

Lionesses in a pride often come into breeding condition at the same time, so a lot of cubs are born at once. Strangely, a majority of these newborn cubs are male.

Male lions are more likely to succeed in life if they have brothers and cousins of the same age. They can leave the pride together in a big group, take over another pride, and produce cubs of their own.

A lioness is likely to have more descendants if she has her male cubs at the same time as her sisters produce their own cubs. Exactly why so many male cubs are born at the same time is a mystery, although it is possible that the extra males are identical twins.

Cubs

A lioness carries her babies inside her for 14 to 15 weeks. She gives birth to two or three cubs, which weigh from 2 to 4 pounds (0.9 to 1.8kg). The newborn cubs are blind and helpless.

The mother goes to a quiet place to have her cubs and hides them carefully before leaving to join the other lionesses in the hunt. She returns to feed the cubs on her milk.

The cubs' eyes open when they are between three and eleven days old. They start to walk after about two weeks. They stay hidden, though, and always slip out of sight at the slightest alarm. It may be another month or more before they are ready to join the rest of the pride.

The lionesses in the pride help look after each others' cubs and even feed them on their milk.

▲ *These young lions are learning hunting skills by attacking their mother. This type of play fighting provides valuable training for when they are older.*

Spotty cubs

Adult lions are tawny yellow; but when they are born, the cubs are covered with dark spots. These markings help protect them from enemies by acting as camouflage in the dappled shade of their hiding places. The spots start to fade at the age of three months and then usually disappear altogether.

Gradually the young lions learn to take solid food, and by the age of three months they are playing at stalking their own prey.

Dangerous days

Eight out of ten lion cubs die before they are two years old. The newborn cubs are no bigger than rabbits; and if they are not well hidden or defended, they make easy prey for eagles, hyenas, and other killers. If prey is scarce, the youngsters are also likely to starve. The biggest threat to cubs, though, is other lions: killer males who may drive out their fathers and take over the pride.

Playing is not the real thing, though; and when they join the pride on a serious hunt, the youngsters often scare off the prey by treating the whole thing as a game. The cubs start to take part in hunts when they are about 11 months old. After about 18 months the young lions are ready to look out for themselves.

▲ Lion cubs drinking their mother's milk. The cubs suckle until they are six months old.

▼ A young cub playfully nips a male's rear.

Marauding males

As their manes begin to grow at the age of two and a half, young male lions are forced to leave the pride by the adult males. If they are lucky, three or four leave together, maybe more. Lone males have a struggle to survive and often team up with others. The bigger the gang, the better their chances.

The male lions wander for two or three years, often following migrating herds of antelope and zebra, until they become fully mature at the age of five. At this age they are in their prime. They are big, strong, and fit; and if they run into a pride defended by older, weaker males, they will attack it.

The fights can be savage, and losers are sometimes killed. The young males may be beaten back; but if they win, they drive out the pride males, who then become wanderers themselves. Meanwhile, the victors take over their territory, the pride lionesses, and their cubs, sometimes with terrible consequences.

Keeping control

A strong band of male lions may keep control of a pride for four years or more, but a group of two or three is lucky to last two years. This is just long enough to raise one generation of cubs. If the males are driven out any earlier, they could lose all their cubs to the next gang of males, and all the effort of breeding is wasted. For both males and females it pays to be part of a strong pride.

▶ *The male on the left of this picture is being driven away by a larger rival.*

▼ *Young male and female lions in Chobe National Park, Botswana. Males may stay with their pride for up to six years, but eventually they all leave.*

For a male lion the most important thing in life is fathering cubs. If a new male takes over a pride, he wants the lionesses to raise *his* cubs, not the cubs fathered by the males he has just defeated. He gets rid of the cubs by killing them.

Sometimes the lionesses defend their cubs by joining forces and attacking the murdering males. This is very dangerous, though, and usually the lionesses have to put up with the situation. Once the males settle into their new role as fathers, their cubs are safe—until the next takeover.

Lionesses

Lion society is centred on the females. The pride is really a family group of related lionesses–grandmothers, mothers, and daughters–who live together for many generations.

A young lioness has a much safer life than her brothers because she normally stays in the pride with her mother, sisters, and female cousins. Since all the cubs are brought up together, there is no real pecking order, although some individuals are first in line at kills. The lions in a pride look after each other, and the young lioness learns to do the same.

When she gets old enough, she joins the other lionesses on hunting trips. It can be risky work, especially if they are hunting big animals like zebra. It is a lot less dangerous than

▲ *A group of lionesses takes a much-needed drink at a waterhole. There are usually between four and twelve lionesses in a pride.*

fighting other lions, though, and this is one reason why there are always more adult females than males. Female lions live longer than males. They can live to be 18 years old, while males usually live to 12 years if they have not been killed in a fight before then.

A lioness begins breeding at the age of four. By this time her father has usually been driven from the pride by a male takeover, and one of the new pride males becomes the father of her cubs. A female lion can give birth to a new litter every 18 to 26 months. She may have another four litters of cubs before she becomes too old to breed.

▼ *The life of a pride lioness is much more active than that of a male. She shares the duties of finding food and rearing the young with the other lionesses.*

Thrown out

If a pride grows too big for its territory, some of the young lionesses may have to leave. They wander like young males, and like them they stand a better chance of surviving if they travel in company. Many die young, but a few get accepted into other prides that are short of breeding females. Some start their own prides by mating with wandering males and producing daughters who stay with them for life.

Heavyweight hunter

A lion is a powerhouse killer. Hunting alone, it can kill animals that are four times its own weight. Most cats hunt animals that are smaller than they are because they do not have the power or the weapons to deal with anything bigger. A lion has both.

For one thing, a lion weighs a lot. A male can weigh anything up to 530 pounds (240kg), and even a sleek lioness usually weighs more than 300 pounds (136kg). The weight slows it down; but when a lion leaps on its target, the collision can send the victim sprawling.

The lion uses its teeth to finish off its prey. Like other hunters, it is armed with long, pointed canine teeth, but its jaws are shorter than most.

▼ *In a pride the females provide the food, but a lone male lion has to fend for himself.*

Eyes and ears

A hunting lion relies on its eyes and ears. It can see well even by starlight thanks to a mirrorlike membrane in each eye that reflects light into the light-sensitive cells at the back of the eye. Sound is less important than sight. The prey is usually in view, so a lion does not need to locate it by sound. It still uses its ears a lot, though, especially at night.

This gives its jaw muscles more leverage, so they can squeeze their teeth together with immense force.

When it has made its kill, the lion can start slicing up the body with its bladelike cheek teeth (carnassials). They are specially adapted to shear through skin, flesh, and sinew like scissors. When most of the meat is gone, the lion uses its rasping tongue to scrape the bones clean.

▶ *A lion's skull showing its teeth. The sharp canine teeth at the front act like daggers to kill prey. The scissorlike carnassials in the cheeks shear through the flesh.*

Canines

Paws and claws

Claw retracted

Claw extended

A lion keeps its claws retracted into protective sheaths. This means its claws stay needle-sharp. They make fearful weapons, able to inflict terrible wounds on prey and on other lions.

Carnassials

Big brother

Most male and female cats look very similar, but with lions the difference is obvious. Compared to his sister, an adult male is a hairy giant. He may weigh up to half as much again; and when he wants a meal, he can push a lioness aside with no trouble at all.

In some ways the male's extra weight is a problem. He is less agile than a lioness and cannot run as fast. His big mane may look impressive, but it makes him easier to spot when he is creeping up on prey. This makes him less efficient at stalking and catching prey, and pride males usually leave all the hunting to the lionesses.

Why are males so big? Simply because a small male would stand no chance against rivals trying to take over the pride. The biggest, strongest males always win. Since the winners father all the cubs, the next generation of males is usually big and strong, too. Over time this has created bigger and bigger males, ideally equipped for fighting—if not for hunting.

▲ *Male lions are much heavier than females. A fully grown male weighs around 416 pounds (189kg), while his sister is about 277 pounds (126kg).*

The lion's mane

The most spectacular difference between a lion and a lioness is the male's mane. The mane starts to grow when a lion is about two years old. It looks magnificent, and it is meant to. Males spend a lot of time trying to scare rival males off their territory, preferably without risking a fight; so the bigger and meaner they look, the better. Extra weight helps, but it can be a problem too. A big, bushy mane makes a lion look big without giving it a lot of extra weight.

Despite this, males in some regions do not grow manes. They seem to manage quite well without them, perhaps because none of their rivals have manes either.

▲ The lioness is strong and sleek. Her muscular hindquarters provide power for sprinting, and her strong forelimbs can bring down prey with a single blow.

▼ As well as making the lion look bigger, the flowing mane protects his neck during fights with other lions.

Scissor teeth

The lion is a type of mammal called a carnivore. The word usually means "meat-eater," but it has a different meaning, too. Zoologists use it to describe the group of mammals that includes the cats, dogs, weasels, bears, raccoons, civets, and hyenas.

In general carnivores are all adapted to eat meat, and many are fierce hunters. Some eat other things as well, though, and a few, like the giant panda, are almost entirely vegetarian. One feature that most carnivores share is scissorlike cheek teeth called carnassials. They use them to slice through meat. These shearing teeth are biggest and sharpest in the cats, which are the most dedicated meat-eaters.

Other carnivores have chewing teeth behind the carnassials, but cats have lost them. As a result, a cat has a shorter muzzle than a

► *The jaguar lives in the rainforests of South America. It is equally at home in trees and on the forest floor.*

Meet the family

There are big cats and small cats. They are all built in much the same way, but big cats can roar, while small cats cannot. All cats are hunters, but some are very specialized. The cheetah, for example, chases its prey like a greyhound, and the margay of South America hunts up in the trees. Most of the other cats are stealth killers that ambush their victims. The lion is the only type of cat that hunts in groups.

dog or a bear and a more powerful killing bite.

Only one cat is more powerful than a male lion—the tiger. A male Siberian tiger can weigh up to 750 pounds (360kg). It is a formidable killer, able to bring down big prey without the help of a pride. That is partly because it lives in forests, where there is plenty of cover. A hunting tiger can creep up close to its victim and pounce before it has a chance to escape—and it gets to eat the whole carcass itself.

▶ *The Siberian tiger is the biggest of the big cats. This very rare animal lives in northern China and Russia.*

Habitat

Lions are open-country cats. They hunt grazing animals, and to do so they must follow the herds across the grasslands.

The open landscape makes life difficult for hunters that stalk their prey because there is nowhere to hide. Lions get around this problem by hunting in groups. This allows lions to survive in some of the most open landscapes in Africa, including the parched savannas of the Serengeti in the east and the Kalahari Desert in the south.

On these dry, grassy plains lions often have to wander across huge areas to find enough prey. Hunting is easier in more wooded landscapes, and ideal lion country is lush grassland with plenty of scrub and shady trees.

The only wild lions surviving outside Africa today live in the Gir Forest of northwest India. There are only about 250 of

▼ *A pride of lions relaxes after a kill. This is an ideal lion landscape. The trees and bushes hide the lions from their prey and shelter them from the baking African sun.*

Shrinking horizons

We think of lions as African, but they were once widespread through southern Asia and Europe. The legend of Hercules describes him fighting lions in Greece. Lions roamed the deserts of the Middle East only 100 years ago, and there are still a few in India. Today lions are even disappearing from Africa. Over the last 100 years about half of Africa's lions have been hunted and killed. Many of the ones that are left cannot find enough to eat because much of the lion's habitat has been turned into farmland. Soon the only places left for lions will be wildlife reserves.

▲ The Gir Forest was turned into a wildlife sanctuary in 1965, mainly to protect the remaining Asiatic lions. It is the only place where Asiatic lions live in the wild.

◄ Areas where African and Asian lions live.

them, living in a wildlife sanctuary that covers 386 square miles (1,000 sq km) of grassland and forest. Since they can ambush prey from forest cover, like tigers, group-hunting tactics are not so important. Prides are smaller than those of the African lion, with two males and three or four females. They are now protected by law, but there are so few of them that their future is uncertain.

Lions and people

Two thousand years ago the Romans were importing lions from North Africa for their wild beast shows. As part of the entertainment, criminals were thrown to the lions to be killed and even eaten. These grisly exhibitions took place in open-air theatres called circuses.

As time went on, circuses became less violent, but lions were still a big attraction. Lion-tamers trained lions to perform tricks, and between shows the animals lived in cramped cages. Meanwhile, other lions were displayed in zoos, also in small cages. Even if they were well cared for—and many were not—it was nothing like their life in the wild.

Today most lions in zoos are kept in large enclosures where they have grass, trees, and space. In some North American zoos lions are being bred in captivity in case they die out in the wild. Many wild lions live in African wildlife reserves and national parks, where they are protected from hunters. Reserves include the Serengeti and Kalahari Gemsbok National Parks. These parks cover vast areas of grassland and forest, allowing their resident lions to live wild and free.

Big game

In the distant past killing a lion was a real act of bravery. Then the rifle was invented, and anyone could do it. For some reason, though, shooting a lion was still something to be proud of, and "big game hunting" became very popular among the rich and famous. Luckily, hunting is now controlled in the national parks, and people travel to Africa to photograph lions rather than to shoot them.

◄ *Many places now ban circuses with animals. Modern circuses are more likely to use human skills.*

▲ *Lions are an important tourist attraction in African wildlife reserves and national parks.*

"Maneaters"

Wild lions often attack farm animals, especially where their normal prey is scarce; but human-eating lions are rare. This is odd because people are soft targets. They are slow, easy to stalk, and no trouble to kill. The few lions that regularly kill people are usually too old and feeble to kill anything else.

Further reading

Amazing Cats
by Alexander Parsons
(Alfred Knopf, 1990).

Big Cats
by Norman Barrett
(Franklin Watts, 1990).

Big Cats
by Douglas Richardson
(Whittet Books, 1992).

Cats of Africa
by Anthony Hall-Martin
and Paul Bosman
(Smithsonian Institution
Press, 1998).

In the Lion's Den
by Mitsuaki Iwago
(Chronicle Books, 1995).

Kingdom of Lions
by Jonathon Scott
(Rodale Press, 1995).

**The Lion: Habitats,
Life Cycles, Food
Chains, Threats**
by Bill Jordan
(Raintree/Steck-
Vaughn, 1999).

Lions
by Brian Bertram
(Voyager Press, 1998).

Lions
by Leslie McGuire
(Atheneum, 1989).

Lions, King of Beasts
by Lee Server
(Longmeadow Press, 1993).

The Mountain Lion
by Rebecca Grambo and
Daniel Cox (Chronicle
Books, 1999).

Wild Cats of the World
by Art Wolfe and Barbara
Sleeper (1995).

Web sites

www.geocities.com
www.ic.arizona.edu
www.lionresearch.org
www.nature-wildlife.com
www.ops.org

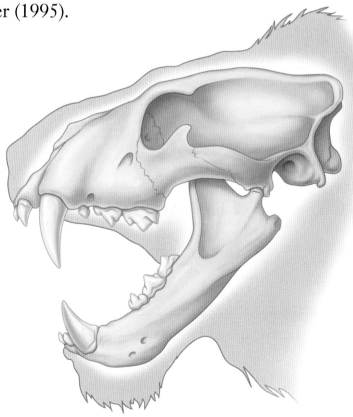

Glossary

camouflage: the markings or colours on an animal that make it more difficult for enemies to see.

carnassial: a very sharp, bladelike tooth used for cutting meat.

carnivore: a large group of meat-eating animals that includes cats, dogs, bears, weasels, and lions.

cub: a baby or young lion.

estrus: the state when a lioness can become pregnant.

habitat: the kind of place where a particular animal lives.

lioness: a female lion.

mammal: a kind of animal that is warm-blooded and has a backbone. Most are covered with fur. Females have glands that produce milk to feed their young.

mane: the long fur that grows around an adult male lion's neck.

mate: when a male and female get together to produce young.

muzzle: the part of an animal's face that sticks out; usually its jaws and nose.

pride: a family group of lions.

range: the parts of the world in which a particular type of animal can be found.

retracted: when a lion's claws are drawn back into its paws.

savanna: open grasslands with scattered bushes and trees.

territory: the area over which a pride of lions ranges.

tropical: having to do with or found within the tropics.

Index